# Praying God's Word

# Praying God's Word

The key that will unlock every door
The effectual fervent prayer of a
righteous man availeth much. James 5:16

Barbara Taylor, Ph.D

XULON PRESS

Xulon Press
2301 Lucien Way #415
Maitland, FL 32751
407.339.4217
www.xulonpress.com

© 2020 by Barbara Taylor, Ph.D

All rights reserved solely by the author. The author guarantees all contents are original and do not infringe upon the legal rights of any other person or work. No part of this book may be reproduced in any form without the permission of the author. The views expressed in this book are not necessarily those of the publisher.

Unless otherwise indicated, Scripture quotations taken from the King James Version (KJV)–*public domain.*

Printed in the United States of America.

ISBN-13: 978-1-6628-0670-4
Ebook ISBN-13: 978-1-6628-0671-1

# Table of Contents

The Lord's Prayer.....................................1
Daily Prayer ........................................1
Healing ........................................... 2
Finances .......................................... 3
For the Holy Ghost ............................... 4
Hunger for God .................................. 5
Depression ....................................... 5
Loneliness........................................ 6
Broken Hearted ...................................7
When You Have Been Miss-Understood ..............7
For Business Success............................... 8
For Husband ...................................... 8
For Wife ......................................... 9
Troubled Marriage ............................... 10
For Children .................................... 10
For Addictions .................................. 11
For Grief........................................ 12
For Success in Life .............................. 12

# Introduction

We bring so much before God in the form of prayer. We bring ourselves, spouses, significant others, children, jobs, problems with other people, problems with vehicles, and so on and so on. Many times, we do not see the results from prayer that we desire to see. Often times, we pray amiss and miss God. When we pray out of the will of God, our prayers will not produce the result that we are seeking. We must begin to pray prayers, that will move the hand of God.

When we begin to pray God's Word, God will honor His Word in our lives. When everything else fails, His Word will remains with truth. According to **Matthew 24:35**, *"Heaven and earth; shall pass away, but my words shall not pass away."* His Word will be honored in the heavens and in the earth. According to **Hebrews 5:7,8,** Jesus offered up prayers and petitions with loud cries and tears to God. The only one who could save him from death. Jesus' prayers were heard, not only because he was the Son of God, but due to his obedience to his Father and his total submission to God's will. Yet, being the Son of God, Jesus learned obedience from what he suffered."

If Jesus prayed and God answered his prayers, God will answer your prayers. Many have prayed and feel that God has not answered their prayers. According to **John 9:31**, "*Now we know that God heareth not sinners; but if any man be a worshipper of God, and doeth his will, him he heareth.*" Our first prayer, should be the prayer of repentance. Clear the slat that your prayers be no hindered. Don't allow Satan to deceive you in your thinking that you have no sin. **1 John 1:8,9**, tell us "*If we claim to be without sin, we deceive ourselves and the truth is not in us. If we confess our sins, he is faithful and just and will forgive us our sins and purify us from all unrighteousness.*" God will hear a sinner's prayer of repentance. As stated in **Hosea 14:1 ,2**; " *Return, O Israel, to the Lord your God. Your sins have been your downfall! Take words with you and return to the Lord. Say to him: "Forgive all our sins and receive us graciously, that we may offer the fruit of our lips.*" (NIV)

## What is Prayer?

Prayer, (*Greek; Proseuch*), is *"communion with God"*. Through prayer we actually experience relationship with God. The quality of our prayer life then determines the quality of our relationship with God. In short, prayer is talking with God and listening to God. Prayer is entering and enjoying God's presence.

## Why Pray?

- **We love God**, we communicate with those we love and seek to please them. Deuteronomy 11:22 NIV; "if you carefully observe all these commands I am giving you to follow-to love the Lord you God to walk in all his ways and to hold fast to him".
- **We depend on God for all our needs.** If we consult him in all our ways, he will not lead us wrong. Psalm 62:7 NIV; "My salvation and my honor depend on God; he is my mighty rock, my refuge."
- **To resist temptation.** Prayer keeps us strong. Lack of prayer promotes spiritual weakness and gives Satan the upper hand. Scripture tells us; Luke 18:1; "Man should always pray, lest he faint".

- **God commands us to pray.** "*Pray without ceasing.*" (**1 Thessalonians 5:17**). Pray is so vital, that God commands us to do it all the time.
- **For Change.** Something are not going to change, some things are not going to happen unless God does it. We have not because we ask not. **Matthew 7:7;** "*Ask and you shall receive, seek and you shall find, knock and the door shall be opened unto you.*" Asking, seeking and knocking is done through prayer.

**How to Pray?**

- **Thanksgiving.** Come before God with a heart of thanksgiving. Giving thanks for who He is and for what He is able to do.
- **Love.** Share with God how much you love Him. Assure Him that you love Him more than life itself. Besides Him, nothing else matters.
- **Forgiveness.** Repent of everything you have done, said and even thought, that was not in the will of God. Things that you were aware of and even things you weren't aware of. Seek forgiveness for those you may have hurt through words or deeds (aware/unaware).
- **Ask.** Make your request known to God. Ask Him for what you will. The slate is clean.

- **Pray His Word.** Give back to God His Word in prayer. Praying His word will avoid praying amiss. Praying His word will result in more answered prayers. God has made promises to us through His word. God will keep His promises. Example: *Pray, "Father, you said in your Word, that those who seek you will not lack any good thing. Father, I seek you with my whole heart, and I thank you that is no lack in my life. I ask you for this in Jesus' name. Thank you for it. Amen." (Psalm 34:10). Guaranteed results.*
- **In Jesus Name.** Always ask in the name of Jesus. This is the password to the heart of God. **John 14:13, 14** *"And whatsoever ye shall ask in my name, that will I do, that the Father may be glorified in the Son. If ye shall ask any thing in my name I will do it."*

# Prayers

*Praying God's Word*

**The Lord's Prayer**

Our Father, who art in heaven, hallowed be thy name. Thy kingdom come; Thy will be done, on earth as it is in heaven. Give us this day our daily bread, and forgive us our trespasses, as we forgive those who trespass against us. And lead us not into temptation, but deliver us from evil. For Thine is the kingdom, and the power, and the glory, forever and ever. Amen
**Matthew 6:9-13.**

**Daily Prayer**

Father God in the name of Jesus I thank and praise you for being God. You are the God of my life, my spirit and my soul. I thank you for this day. For this is the day that you have made and I am rejoicing and I'm glad in it. I pray that you take control of this day. Have your way in everything that I say and do. I pray that my actions today will glorify you in you majesty. Father, bless me and all that I venture to do this day. Bless the works of my hands and my goings. Sharpen my gifts that they may be used for your glory. Father, grant me wisdom and favor from on high. Father, I pray that you will watch over my family, possessions, and business. I pray that you will cover all that concerns me in the blood of Jesus. Let no evil befall us. Father, I pray this prayer in the name of Jesus. And it is so! Amen

## Healing

Father God, in the name of Jesus, I thank you for being my God of divine health. I bring to you now, my afflictions, infirmities, diseases, and (name your condition). I know that there is nothing too hard for you. I release my faith to embrace your word, that will usher in the healing that I stand in need of. Faith, embrace **Isaiah 53:5:** *"He was wounded for MY transgressions, he was bruised for MY iniquities: the chastisement of MY peace was upon him; and with his stripes I am healed,"* Father I praise you for **3 John 2;** *"Beloved, I wish above all things that thou mayest prosper and be in health, even as MY soul prospereth."* I now walk in divine health in Jesus name! Amen

Father God, in the name of Jesus, I present to you (name the illness/injury). You are the healer of healers. You are my God. Father, heal me and deliver me from (name the illness/injury) and restore my health as you said you would in **Jeremiah 30:17;** *"For I will restore health unto thee, and I will heal thee of thy wounds, saith the Lord."* Father, I trust you to do this for me in Jesus name. Amen

**Finances**

Father God, in the name of Jesus, I thank you for being my God of finances. It is not your will for my life that I need and my needs be not met. It is not your will for my life that I want and my wants be not met. Father, I release my faith to embrace **Philippians 4:19**, *"But my God shall supply all MY need according to his riches in glory by Christ Jesus."* Therefore, there is nothing that I need that you, my God can not provide. I walk by **Matthew 6:33,** *"But seek ye first the kingdom of God, and his righteousness; and all these things shall be added unto you."* Therefore, whatsoever I need and desire is automatically added unto me. Father, I praise you for **Psalm 37:4**, *"Delight thyself also in the Lord; and he shall give ME the desires of MY heart."* Thank you God for honoring your Word in my life and releasing unto me those things that I stand in need of and desire. In Jesus Name! Amen

Father God, in the name of Jesus, I thank you for being my God of finances and resources. I had a need for (*name your need*) and I hold fast to **Psalms 23:1**, "*The Lord is my shepherd: I shall not want.*" Father I release my faith to embrace these words and quickly bring unto me that which I stand in need of in the name of Jesus. I now rejoice, because my need for (*name your need*) is already done in Jesus name! Amen

**For the Holy Spirit**

**Acts 1:5 NIV**; *For John baptized with water, but in a few days you will be baptized with the Holy Spirit."*
**Acts 1:8 NIV**; *But you will receive power when the Holy Spirit comes on you; and you will be my witnesses in Jerusalem, and in all Judea and Samaria, and to the ends of the earth."*
**Acts 2:4 NIV**; *All of them were filled with the Holy Spirit and began to speak in other tongues as the Spirit enabled them.*
**Acts 2:38 NIV**; *and be baptized, every one of you, in the name of Jesus Christ for the forgiveness of your sins. And you will receive the gift of the Holy Spirit.*

Father, before Jesus ascended into heaven, You promised to send the Holy Spirit to Your apostles and disciples. Grant me the same Spirit that will make perfect in my life the works of your grace and love. Father forgive me of all my sins and fill my temple with the precious gift of the Holy Spirit. Grant the me the power that comes with the filling of the Holy Spirit, that I may have power over all demons, disease and forms of sickness, in Jesus name. Father, I thank you for hearing and answering my prayer, now in Jesus name. Amen

**Hunger for God**

Father God, just "*as the hart panteth after the water brooks, so panteth my soul after thee, O God.* " **Psalm 42:1**. Father, my soul hungers and longeth for more of you. I have a hunger and a thirst that only you can satisfy. I believe your Word, **Psalm 107:9**; "*For he (you my God) satisfieth the longing soul, and filleth the hungry soul with goodness.*" Father, fill my heart with your Word and satisfy my soul with your spirit. Father, bring forth **Matthew 5:6** greatly in my life, "*Blessed are they which do hunger and thirst after righteousness: for they shall be filled.*" Thank you God for satisfying my soul. Thank you God for satisfying my life, in Jesus name. Amen

**Depression**

Father, I come unto just as I am. I need a touch from your healing hand. Father, life has tossed me into a place where, I am now left perplexed and depressed. I am standing on **Psalm 34: 15, 17**; where your word tells me, "*The eyes of* the Lord are upon the righteous, and his ears are open unto their cry. The righteous cry, and the Lord heareth, and delivereth them out of all their troubles." Father, I am crying for deliverance from this depression. I can not handle this, but you can. I give it to you now. Father, *I cast all my cares upon you, for you careth for me* (**I Peter 5:7**). I trust you Father to free me now from depression in Jesus name. Amen

## Loneliness

Father, I am reminded of your Word: "*I will not leave you comfortless; I will come to you.*" **John 14:18** Father, I need to feel your presence today. I am troubled with the feeling of loneliness. I ask to feel your love and comfort. I know you have not forsaken me, I believe your word according to **Deuteronomy 31:6**; "*Be strong and of a good courage, fear not, nor be afraid of them; for the Lord thy God, he it is that doth go with thee; he will not fail thee, nor forsake thee.*" I stand strongly upon **Psalm 27:10**; "*When my father and my mother forsake me then the Lord will take me up.*" Father, I know that you are closer than you have ever been. I pray that you will deliver me now from loneliness and make me whole in Jesus name. Thank God, Amen

## Broken Hearted

Father, I praise you for being the healer of my brokenness. As I come before you with my broken heart, I pray **Psalm 147:3**; *"He healeth the broken in heart, and bindeth up their wounds"*. Father, heal my broken hearth and bind up all my wounds. I know you are able to deliver me from all that afflicts my heart and my spirit. I give my brokenness to you, so that you will heal all that concerneth me. Thank you Father, for healing and delivering me in Jesus name. And so it is, in Jesus name. Amen

## When You Have Been Miss-Understood

Father, I come to you now, because you know the way that I take. Your Word tells me that *"the Lord knoweth the way of the righteous"*. **Psalm 1:6** I have attempted to do good, and my good has been misunderstood. I have tried to love and my love has been taken for granted. I have walked in your way, and those that say the believe with me have now walked away from me. Father, this hurts. Take away this hurt, that I feel in my heart and my spirit. Restore my joy and my peace as I continue my walk in your way. Father, help me to feel no more pain. Help me to feel no more rejection. Help me to continue to love as you love in Jesus name. Father, I thank you now for the overflow of your joy and peace that I am feeling right now. Thank you Father, for helping me in Jesus name. Amen

## For Business Success

Father, I thank you for (*name of business*). This is the manifestation of your divine plan for my life. I cherish (*name of business*) because it is an avenue of income for me as well as an avenue for you to demonstrate your glory. Father, I pray that you will bring great success to (*name of business*) as it carries out it's purpose. Father you said in your Word that you will bless that which I puteth my hands to". Thank you Father, for blessing (*name of business*). Thank you for the souls that will be reached and won through (*name of business*). Thank you for the great success and prosperity of (*name of business*), in Jesus name. Amen

## For Husband

Father, I thank you for my husband, (*name of spouse*). For this is the husband that you have given unto me as my head and covering. I reverence my husband for he is a man after your heart. Father, I pray that you will bless (*name of spouse*) to be the husband and father, that you have purposed him to be. Bless him with the resources that he needs and desire to have that will enable him to provide sufficiently for his family. Father, as he walks in your will, grant him the very desires of his heart in the name of Jesus. Father, thank you for strengthening (*name of spouse*) to perform the tasks that are set before him. Strengthen him as he continues to walk in your way and remain in your will in Jesus name. I pray Father, that you will help (*name of spouse*) to be all that he can be and all that he desires to become in Jesus name. And it is so! Amen

**For Wife**

Father, I thank you for my wife, (*name of spouse*). For your Word tells me that, "he that findeth a wife findeth a good thing and obtainth favor from the Lord". Father, I thank you for my good thing. You have given me your best and I am most grateful. Thank you. Father, I pray that you bless my wife to be and do all that you have purposed her to be and do. Father, bless that which she puts her hands to. Father, I pray that you will cause her to be blessed in all that she does. Help her to be the wife and mother that she is endeavoring to become. Most of all, Father, strengthen her walk in you. Help her to be the servant that you are calling for today. As she blesses you with her praise, bless her with all that you have for her in Jesus name. Amen

**Troubled Marriage**

Father, I lift thank you for marriage, for marriage is honorable and the bed is undefiled. You said in your word, that every man should have his own wife and every woman her own husband. And we know that Satan has a regime against marriage, for it is the will of Satan that men fall into sin. Father I know that marriages are under attack, therefore, I pray and lift up trouble marriages before you. Father, look down up every marriage and that is under the covenant of your will. Father, shine your grace upon marriages that you have joined together, and allow no man the power to put asunder. Father, I pray that you make right everything that is wrong, and fix everything that is broken, move that which needs to be moved and cause these marriages to line up with your will. Father, I ask that you will all forgiveness to flow between husband and wife. Father, bind them together with your love. The love that Jesus has for the church, allow husbands and wives to love each other unconditional in Jesus name. Thank you Father, for healing every trouble marriage in Jesus name. Amen

**For Children**

Father, I thank you for my children and the children every where. I pray that you will cover my children with the blood of Jesus. Protect them from all hurt, harm and danger, danger seen and unseen. Father, keep them healthy, wealthy, strong and happy in Jesus name. Lord direct the path and order the steps of my children. Father, save (*name the children*) and cause them to live according to your will for their lives,. Father, prepare my children for the education, career, and the spouse you have prepared for them. Father, as you have entrusted them into my hands, I give them back to you to be used for your glory, in Jesus name. Thank you for the gift of my children. Thank you for keeping them, covering them, saving them, shielding them for your glory. In Jesus name. Amen

**For Addictions**

Father I come before you, asking for forgiveness from the things that I have indulged in and became habit forming. I ask in Jesus name that you will deliver me from these things that hold me bound and captive. I denounce (*name the addiction*) from my life and I declare my deliverance in Jesus name. These things will no longer serve as stumbling blocks, but stepping stones in my life. No longer will these things cause me to be a slave to addictions, but I am free according to 1Thessalonians 5:22-23. I will abstain from all appearance of evil. And the very God of my peace will sanctify me wholly; and that my spirit, soul and body be preserved blameless unto the coming of my Lord Jesus Christ. I declare my freedom. I declare my happiness. I declare my restoration. I declare my new life in Christ Jesus. And it is so, in Jesus name. Amen

**For Grief**

Father, I thank you now for the grief that you have allowed to enter into my life. I know without it, I would not know how you are able to remove it from my life. Without it, I would not run to you in the manner in which I run. Without the tears this grief has caused, my eyes have been washed and I see clearly now your power. According to Proverbs 3:5-6, I am able to "Trust in the Lord with all thine (my) heart; and lean not unto thine (my) own understanding. In all thy (my) ways acknowledge him, and he shall direct thy (my) paths. Father, I now trust you with my life and the path that I'm to venture. I pray now, that you God, will remove this grief from my heart, spirit and mind. I pray that you will replace it with the abundance of your love, joy, peace and happiness, in Jesus name. Now, I praise you God for doing it and I call it done in Jesus name. Amen

**For Success in Life**

Father, I thank you for the power of your Word. According to Psalm 1:1-3, *"Blessed is the man that walketh not in the counsel of the ungodly, nor standeth in the way of sinners, nor sitteth in the seat of the scornful.*

*But his delight is in the law of the LORD; and in his law doth he meditate day and night.*

*And he shall be like a tree planted by the rivers of water, that bringeth forth his fruit in his season; his leaf also shall not wither; and whatsoever he doeth shall prosper.*

The blessing of these words rest over my life. The blessing of this promise, is made unto me. As, I abide in your Word and your Word abide in me, I can ask that I will and it shall be done unto me. I ask in faith, for a successful life. I pray success upon all of my endeavors and my aspirations. Father, I thank you for your Word that leads me to success. I thank you for your word that makes me the head and not the tail, above only and never beneath, first and not last. I thank you Father, that now is my time and time has become my turn. Thank you Father, for this life of success in Jesus name. And it is so! Amen

Family New Life Ministries
P.O. Box 310 Spencerville, MD 20868
Pastor Barbara Taylor, Ph.D

I pray that this booklet has been a blessing to you as you endeavor to grow in prayer. As your prayer life grows, you will begin to experience God answering your prayers with natural manifestation. James 5:16 tells us: *Confess your faults one to another, and pray one for another, that ye may be healed. The effectual fervent prayer of a righteous man availeth much.*

Your prayers have much power. Don't stop praying.

CPSIA information can be obtained
at www.ICGtesting.com
Printed in the USA
BVHW081159210321
603030BV00007B/1526